Poetic Musings

By

Yoav J. Tenembaum

©Yoav J. Tenembaum
ISBN: 978-1-918264-81-4
Copyright
2025

Preface

A compilation of personal musings, conveyed in the form of poems, this book is conceptual in content and poetic in both structure and rhythm. The poems touch on various themes, from memory to imagination, from history to philosophy, from anxiety to pain, and from doubt to envy. They combine earnestness with humour, and irony with tenderness. Aimed at a wide readership, the book deals with the personal and the universal and dwells on the particular and the general. The poems are not titled, but are numbered. In total, there are seventy-seven poetic musings.

1.

My room is the airport
From which my imagination
Takes off to the distant
Lands of history,
Overflying some periods
And landing on others
For a brief visit.

2.

Do words depict reality
Or is reality merely
A mirror reflecting
The words we use?

3.

How many opportunities
Have I missed
By not wearing
The right glasses?
How many words
Have I ignored?
How many images
Have I overlooked?
Opportunities come and go,
Glasses don't.

4.

Some people have their own
Bermuda Triangle
In which ideas fade
And memories disappear
Without leaving
A trace behind.

5.

Is harmony caused
By an intentional act
Or is it the result
Of a spontaneous process,
A kind of The Big Bang
Leading to harmony?

6.

Poetry is composed
Of a Holy Trinity:
Rhythm, structure
And concept.
Rhythm is the oxygen,
Structure is the body,
And concept is the purpose.
The absence of none
Is sustainable,
For no life is possible
Without oxygen,
No life is tenable
Without a body,
And no life is worth living
Without purpose.

7.

There is no art form
That is superior
To all the others,
For each art form
Is like a different screwdriver
Designed to unscrew
The mysteries of life,
Designed to unveil
That which has been
Concealed from our eyes.

8.

Haiku poetry
Is to the aesthetic soul
What a drop of water
Is to the thirsty animal –
The first taste
That can hardly satisfy,
That craves for more.

9.

I have never known
How it feels to be a father;
I do know how it feels
To be a grandfather.

To me, being a father
Is a distant fact.
Being a grandfather
Is a palpable feeling.

It is like the difference
Between reading about
A beautiful sunrise
Seen from the balcony
Of a hotel
And seeing a beautiful sunrise
From the balcony of one's own
Home.

10.

Poetry is the fusion
Of thought and emotion,
The nest where both dwell
Without needing to leave it
To seek food or shelter.

11.

Is life worth living
Because of what we feel
For other people
Or because of what other people
Feel for us?

12.

Paintings depict.
Pictures reflect.
Fiction describes.
Music resonates.
Sculpture shapes.
Poetry combines
All of the above,
But in small doses.

13.

My grandson and I
Play chess.
I win,
Even when I lose.

My grandson and I
Play chess.
I win – seldom,
Even when I lose – often.

My grandson and I
Play chess.
I win,
Even when I lose.

14.

My granddaughter,
Almost three years old,
Asked her aunt:
"Do you feel
That you don't
Feel well?"

The seed
Of logic,
Pure and simple,
That can never
Appear in a grown-up,
Who would reject it
As illogical and wrong.

15.

Objectivity is not a virtue.
It's a tool -
To know the truth,
To discover it,
And understand it better.

Objectivity is a tool
Employed by subjective
People, and thus susceptible
To the fallacies of subjectivity.

Thus, objectivity
Is no guarantee
Of truth,
And subjective people,
Who may not pretend
To be objective,
Can be right
Without being
Objective.

16.

Feelings are stronger
Than memory.
Contrary to memory,
Feelings cannot be shut away
Outside one's heart.
Memory can be distracted,
Feelings cannot.

17.

The only horizon
One can see
Is in the past.

The horizon
In the past
Is the furthest
Our memory
Or knowledge
Can go.

The horizon
In the future
Is the nearest
Our imagination
Can reach.

18.

Pain is the butler
That opens the door
And leads one slowly
To the study room
Of one's feelings.

19.

If grown-ups
Were endowed
With the soul
Of a child,
Would they be able
To discern
A living soul
In toys
As children are able to?

20.

To fall asleep
One counts sheep.
To remain awake,
I count problems.

21.

One usually
Compares
The present
With the known
Past behind
And not with
The unknown
Future ahead.
That makes
The present
Bearable.

Imagine
The farmer
In the 16th century
Comparing himself
With the farmer
In the 21st century...

Had he known,
Had he seen
The farmer
In the distant
Future,
His present
Would have been
Unbearable.

What makes life
Bearable
Is the fact

That one cannot see
The future,
But only the past.

What makes life
Bearable
Is that one
Can imagine
The future
Without actually
Seeing it.

22.

If the mind
Could erase
A worry
As easily
As an eraser
Can erase
Something written
On a piece of paper
With a pencil,
People would be
More distracted
And less focused.
Isn't that a paradox?

23.

To struggle
With one's
Mind
If one suffers
From OCD
Or anxiety
Is akin
To struggling
With the wind
With toothpicks.

24.

The more autonomy
One grants
To one's mind,
The less autonomy
One has in life.
The less autonomy
One has in life,
The less important
One's mind is.

25.

The mind
Is constructive
When it is
Hardly felt,
And destructive
When it is
Mostly felt.

26.

Imagine a mind
Devoid of
Anything else
But Intellect,
Pure
And
Simple,
With nothing else
But intellect,
No fears,
No obsessions,
No anxieties,
Nothing one's intellect
Cannot conquer,
Nothing one's intellect
Cannot bend to its will.

27.

The problem
With the brain
Is not
What it absorbs,
But rather
What it cannot
Emit.
Contrary
To one's bowel,
The brain
Absorbs
And does not
Emit.

28.

If I do not remember,
Do I forget?

That which I can't remember
Is not necessarily forgotten.

If I do not remember,
I might not have forgotten
That which is hiding
Behind the curtain
Of my memory,
That which eludes
The fishing net
Of my recollections.

29.

The distance between
Reality and fantasy is sometimes akin
To the distance between
The sun and the moon,
Between day and night:
They are separate and different
In light and effect,
But follow one from the other,
Linked in an unbroken
Chain of time.

30.

Sorrow is lighter than a feather,
But it feels heavier than lead,
Pressing strongly on one's chest
And leaving a sense of emptiness
In one's heart.

31.
Like Janus,
Imagination
Has two faces –
One looking
Forward,
The other looking
Backward.
The one looking
Forward
Sees what
Might happen.
The one looking
Backward
Sees what
Did happen.
One depicts
A puzzle
That has yet
To be;
The other
A puzzle
That was.
Thus, the one looking
Forward
Sees opaquely
A constructed puzzle
That might never be
And the one looking
Backward
Sees clearly
The pieces of a puzzle
That was ever there.

32.

The gap
Between
A feeling
Of
Disappointment
And
A feeling
Of
Fulfillment
Can
Sometimes be
Like the gap
Between
One word
And another;
A small,
Even a tiny gap
That separates
Two different
Words
Reflecting
Two opposing
Meanings
And two opposing
Feelings.

33.

Truth
Is there
To be.

It may not
Be visible.

It may be
Difficult
To retrieve.

It may be
Concealed.

But it is
There,
Somewhere,
Waiting
For the door
To open wide
And be seen

Our task
Is to find
That door
And not
Invent
Imaginary
Doors
In its stead
To find

The truth
We want.

34.

Imagine a mind
Without worry...
Imagine a mind
Without anxiety...
Imagine a mind
Without fear...
Now,
Imagine the Earth is flat...

35.

Impartiality
Is not a virtue
And partiality
Is not a vice.
Neither leads
To the truth,
Neither assures
One is right.

Neville Chamberlain
Was impartial in 1938
Between Nazi Germany
And democratic Czechoslovakia.
Edward Benes was not.
Was Chamberlain right?
Was Benes wrong?

Impartiality is a stance,
Not a science.

The further
One is,
The easier
It is to be impartial.
The closer
One is,
The harder
It is to be impartial.
But truth
And
Rightness

Know no distance,
Have no sense
Of time or place.

36.

The pleasure
Of being flattered
Is akin
To the pleasure
Of eating a cheese cake –
Once a month
Would be great.
Once a week
Would be fine.
Once a day
Would be cloying.

37.

Mark Twain
Wrote,
"History
Doesn't repeat itself,
But it often rhymes."
To paraphrase
Mark Twain:
Stupidity
Doesn't repeat itself,
But it often rhymes.

38.

Joseph Heller wrote,
"Just because you
Are paranoid
Doesn't mean
They aren't
After you."
To paraphrase
Joseph Heller:
Just because
You suffer
From anxiety
Doesn't mean
What you fear
Might happen
Won't happen.

39.

People fear
Death
More than
They fear
Nightmares
Because
Death,
Contrary
To nightmares,
Has no
Morning after
To forget.

40.

The way
To prevent
Anxious memories
And
Obsessive thoughts
To kidnap me
Is to hire
Oblivion
To become
My bodyguard.

41.

The concept of eternity
Has never captured
My imagination.
The challenge
Entailed in what
Might actually
Occur to me
In a minute
Or an hour
From now
Has taken hold
Of me,
Leaving precious little
Room
For any reflection
On what might
Take place in a year
Or beyond that.

42.

I find distraction
In assessing the past
Rather than
In divining the future.
I find solace
In gazing
At the past
Rather than
In imagining
The future.
Images
Of the past
May hurt,
But they don't
Awaken fears.
Images
Of the future,
Particularly
The immediate one,
May ignite fear.
The certainty
Of the past
Has a placid effect
Which the uncertainty
Of the future
Can never have.

43.

Time that has elapsed
Will never return,
Like the death
Of a person,
But without
A Funeral.

44.

Amos Oz
Wrote
That
Words
Can be
Lethal
As hand-grenades.

Indeed!

Words
Can be
Soothing
As cotton.

Words
Can be
Rough
As sandpaper.

Words
Can be
Quenching
As water.

Words
Can be
Alarming
As fire.

Words

Can be
All these
And much more.

An endless
Tool
To describe,
To elicit,
To respond,
To hurt,
To heal,
To defend,
To attack,
To kill,
To revive.

Words
Can outlast life.

Men and women,
Animals and plants
Will fade into oblivion,
And words will still
Be there
To fulfill
These ever-lasting
Functions
Irrespective of
Time and place.

45.

Toleration
May be
A virtue
If the alternative
Is persecution.

Toleration
Is not
A virtue
If the alternative
Is mutual respect.

For
Toleration
Entails
An unequal
Relationship
Between
The one tolerating
And the one being tolerated.

Toleration
Denotes an improvement
From a previous condition,
But it becomes a virtue
Only if a better alternative
Is inconceivable
Under prevailing circumstances.

46.

An advantage
Of losing one's memory
Is that one does not miss
A loved one.
But then, if that were the case,
And memory faded into oblivion,
One would not recall the loved one,
To begin with.
The loved one would be like a stranger.
Would you miss a stranger?

47.

Pain is the bell
That reminds
The non-anxious person
Of the existence
Of his or her body.

The anxious person
Needs no bell
For he or she
Carries it
Everywhere.

For whom
Does the bell toll?

48.

What is
The difference
Between
A grown-up's imagination
And
A child's imagination?
A child would see
Imagination
As an extension
Of reality,
Blurring
The distinction
Between
The two,
Amalgamating
Both of them
Like shoelaces.

49.

Imagination
Can be
Constructive
Helping to create,
To devise anew,
Or destructive
Leading to ruin,
Sorrow and pain.

Is imagination
A version of
Jekyll and Hyde,
The same one
With two distinct
And contradictory
Personalities?

50.

Memory
Is like
A full-speed train
That takes me
To my loved ones
In the past.

Imagination
Is like
A full-speed train
That takes me
To my loved ones
In the future.

My loved ones
Are thus able
To link
Memory
And
Imagination
Into one,
Like
The pluot,
A hybrid fruit
Of a plumb
And
An apricot.

51.

Can you imagine
If God had been undecided?
God might still be
On the first day of creation
Unsure whether
To go on
Or
To stop.

52.

In a world
In which everyone
Was undecided,
Everything
Would be in motion
Without actually moving.

53.

Rene Descartes
Wrote, "I think,
Therefore I am."
To paraphrase him
I would write that
"I doubt, therefore
I am."

54.

Rene Descartes
Wrote,
"Doubt is
The origin
Of wisdom."

I would paraphrase him,
"Doubt is
The origin
Of doubt…"

55.

Style
Can have an impact
No less so than content.

Just imagine
Adolf Hitler
With the style
Of Neville Chamberlain...
Or vice versa...
Role reversal
Of style,
Not content.

Would Hitler
Have had
The political
Success
He did?
Would Chamberlain
Have been
Appointed as Prime Minister?

56.

The fact
That X is right
Does not necessarily
Mean that Y is wrong.
There might be
A situation
In which
X and Y
Are both
Right.

This is
Not to say
That one
Has to seek
In a contrived way
A geometrical formula
Entailing a balanced
Philosophy of truth
By which X and Y
Ought to be
Always in a fine
Equilibrium
Between
Truth and truth.

57.

Envy
Is divided
Into two:
Bad envy
And
Good envy.

Bad envy
Is when
You want
The other
To fail.

Good envy
Is when
You want
To succeed
Like the other.

Bad envy
And
Good envy
Have precious
Little to do
With competition.
It is not an active
Endeavour,
But a passive one.
It's a feeling,
Not a plan of action.

58.

If you saw
A new bouquet of flowers,
Would you notice
Which one of those flowers
Suffers from psychological
Or emotional problems?
Would you notice
Which one of those flowers
Suffers from a chronic
Physical problem,
Which is not visible?

Yes, I know, you are
Probably laughing
At my silly questions.

Now,
Let me ask you,
If you saw
A new group of people,
Would you notice
Who among them
Suffers from psychological
Or emotional problems?
Would you notice
Who among them
Suffers from a chronic
Physical problem,
Which is not visible?

Appearances
Know
No distinctions
Between
Nature's creations.

59.

There are
Two kinds
Of change:
Passive change
And
Active Change.

There are
Two kinds
Of passive change:
Change that
Is caused
by biology,
upon which
We have little
Influence,
And change
That is caused
By nature,
Upon which
We have some
Influence.

There are
Two kinds
Of active change:
Change that
Is caused
By others,
And change
That is caused

By oneself.

The most
Challenging
Of them all
Is change
That is caused
By oneself,
For it depends
On having to decide
To change,
Then proceeding
To change,
And then persevering
Until change
Becomes the norm.

60.

One's ego
Can be essential
To survive,
To succeed.

One's ego
Can be detrimental
When it ignores
Somebody else's ego.

One's ego
Can be destructive
When it crushes
Somebody else's ego.

One's ego
Can repel
Without
Ignoring,
Without
Crushing,
Somebody
Else's ego,
Just by pretending
To be bigger
Than the body
It carries.

61.

Arrogance
Is to human-relationship
What extreme heat
Is to fresh food -
The longer it prevails,
The greater the probability
That it will cause
Discomfort and illness.

62.

The individual
Shapes reality
Within the constraints
Of time and place.

History
Does not follow
An inevitable path,
For it is the individual,
Either singly or in groups,
That delineates the road
To be taken,
That defines the objective
To be reached.

Individuals
Do not perform
In a play
Written and directed
By somebody else.

Individuals
Are not pawns
Moved back and forth
By an invisible hand
Playing a game
Of which they
Are not aware.

Deterministic theories
Of history postulating

Events are bound
To happen,
That there is a linear
Historical move
Leading to an inevitable end,
Or
That there is a cyclical
Historical move
Leading to a never-ending
Series of events that keep
Repeating themselves,
Are more literary
Than historical
In nature,
As appealing
As fantasies
And as true
As legends.

63.

Does the individual
Have free will?

Yes.

However,
The range of free will
Enjoyed by the individual
Is circumstantial.

The prisoner's free will
Is more limited
Than the free person's
Outside prison.

Free will exists,
But has precious
Little meaning
If it is divorced
From the conditions
Within which
It is exercised.

64.

History teaches nothing.
It is there to be discovered,
Deciphered, understood,
Interpreted and assessed.
History is a puzzle that needs
Historians to build it into
A coherent whole.

History does not teach.
Historians teach.
People make use
Of history,
For better or for worse,
To learn, to illustrate,
To persuade, to justify,
And to elicit support.

"The lessons of history"
Are nothing more
Than the lessons
Learned from history
By human beings,
And not the lessons
History teaches human beings.

65.

Is life
A metaphor?

If so,
A metaphor for what?

66.

OCD and anxiety
Are able to enrich
One's imagination
More than any
Literary work.

No writer,
However fertile
His or her
Imagination is,
Can deploy
The list of
Problems,
The list of
Ever-changing
Obstacles,
That a person
Might encounter,
And the means
To cope with them,
As someone
With OCD and anxiety can.

67.

There are three Ds
That constitute
The guidelines
Of every academic
Study:

Delineate the framework.
Define the subject.
Describe its nature.

There is an additional D,
Which lurks in the background,
Just in case it is needed...

Do not bother the audience
With superfluous details.

68.

A friend of mine
Once said to me
That boring people
Occupy too much space,
Consume too much oxygen,
At the expense
Of non-boring ones.

His remark
Was not the beginning
Of a joke,
But the end of a story,
A concluding dot
To something
He had told me
About someone else.

69.

The widely accepted notion
That "The truth must be
Somewhere in the middle,"
Is ostensibly appealing,
But logically unsound.

The truth
Is to be found
Where it is,
Not in an imagined
Point between
Two opposing claims.
The truth
Is not a compromise.
A compromise
May be the right
Solution, but not
The signpost
Signaling
Where the truth is.

70.

The spontaneity
Of a child,
The unfeigned
Facial expressions,
The unrehearsed
Manifestations
Of happiness,
The wide-open eyes
Denoting surprise,
Make the child
The Eighth Wonder
Of the World.

71.

What is the ideal sense of equilibrium?

When a person manages
Not to take himself or herself seriously
While being taken seriously by others.

72.

When does the ridiculous embrace the dangerous?

When a person with an exaggerated sense
Of self-importance believes that there is a vacuum
In this world that ought to be filled only by him or her.

When does the dangerous embrace the ridiculous?

When the same person finds no vacuum to fill,
And decides to start digging to create one.

73.

The movie,
"As Good as It Gets,"
Featuring Jack Nicholson
As an unbearably obnoxious
Writer who suffers from OCD,
Implies that being unbearably obnoxious
Is a visible symptom of OCD.

Well, it is not.
A singularly pleasant person
Can suffer from OCD
No less so
Than an unbearably obnoxious
Person.

OCD's reputation
Has been tarnished
By this movie.

OCD should have sued
For character defamation.

74.

A grown-up's vision
Is a fusion
Of a child's imagination
And a grown-up's experience.

75.

Whenever images
Of my grandson
And my granddaughter
Emerge in my mind,
A big smile
And a sense of joy
Ensue.

The Pavlovian effect
Of the heart.

76.

One's life is a federation
Of lives,
Each one having its own
Autonomy,
Linked together by a unifying
Cord
Of family, identity, and personality.

77.

I play hide-and-seek
With OCD.
OCD always
Finds me.

www.ingramcontent.com/pod-product-compliance
Lightning Source LLC
Chambersburg PA
CBHW052111070526
44584CB00017B/2443